D0944163

a gift for us to share

to:..

from:.......................................

OTHER HELEN EXLEY GIFTBOOKS IN THIS SERIES:
Me and my Mum
Me and my Dad
Me and my Grandad

OTHER HELEN EXLEY GIFTBOOKS:
Forever my Grandma
To a very special Grandma
To a lovely Grandma

First published in 2006 by Helen Exley Giftbooks in
Great Britain, and Helen Exley Giftbooks LLC in the USA.
This edition published in 2010.

12 11 10 9 8 7 6 5 4 3 2

Illustrations © Jane Massey 2006, 2010
Copyright © Helen Exley 2006, 2010
The moral right of the author has been asserted.

ISBN 978-1-84634-524-1

Helen Exley Giftbooks,
16 Chalk Hill, Watford,
Herts WD19 4BG, UK.
www.helenexleygiftbooks.com

Me
and my
Grandma

Written by Helen Exley and Illustrated by Jane Massey

My Grandma is kind and soft and gentle. No one else is so kind, not anyone in the whole wide world.

She's never cross. She loves me.

we talk for hours. Boy, can we talk. It takes <u>hours</u> to eat because we tell each other everything. She wants to know what I've done. I tell her my troubles and she's the one person in the world

with time to listen

to everything I need to say.

Grandmas are supposed to grow slow and old, but mine doesn't think so. Her white hairs have all gone and she says she's just starting on the best bits of life now. She says she's an Adventurer - I'm going to be one, too.

When we go shopping my Gran buys me anything I want so I don't dare say when I like something. She shops and shops and we walk and walk and laugh and laugh. Back home she flops down and says "My feet are killing me" and "Ah! Tea at last!"

Grandma calls me "Little One" and silly things like that. And she never thinks I can do anything wrong. She knows absolutely everything about me and my family. She keeps every note I ever write.

My Grandma's home smells lovely. Every time I walk through the door she's been baking things for me. I'm the one who's allowed to lick the mixture off the cake spoon. "Thank you, Grandma. They're my best cakes because they're made by you."

Grandmas are supposed to be polite
and quiet and ladylike. But mine's
just not like that. When we went
on the bumper cars she bumped everyone
in sight and shouted her head off.
She was the naughtiest and the noisiest.

when I told her I was making
something just for her she
started to cry. She also cries
when we say goodbye.

Grandmothers are
like that, you know.

My Grandma has an important job. She is always busy and works very hard. She looks after other people in her job.

She's got time to help everyone - especially me.

She never forgets to speak to me

on my birthday.

when my best Ted was run over
(by our car) he was badly wounded
and torn. So Grandma mended him
washed him, and put him out to dry
She always helps me. Always.

when I have a worry, Grandma
can quietly talk it through.
She wants to help me to grow up
to be a nice person.
Most of all she teaches me
about being kind.

If I had everything in the world
I'd give my Grandma a field of
poppies. I love her so much.

And inside me I know that
she'll love me, forever.

WHAT IS A HELEN EXLEY GIFTBOOK?

Helen Exley Giftbooks cover the most powerful of all
human relationships: the bonds within families
and between friends, and the theme of personal value.
No expense is spared in making sure that each book
is as meaningful a gift as it is possible to create:
good to give, good to receive. You have the result
in your hands. If you have loved it – tell others!
There is no power on earth like the word-of-mouth
recommendation of friends!